WHAT SHE KNEW

WHAT SHE KNEW

PETER FILKINS

ORCHISES
WASHINGTON
1998

Library of Congress Cataloging in Publication Data
Filkins, Peter.
    What she knew / Peter Filkins.
        p. cm.
    ISBN 0-914061-66-6 (alk. paper)
    I. Title.
    PS3556.I4288W48 1998
    811'.54—dc21   97-25370
                              CIP

ACKNOWLEDGMENTS

These poems appeared in these periodicals, some in slightly different form:
Agni: "Traveling in America"; *The American Scholar:* "Hidden Meadow"
and "Just"; *Atlanta Review:* "Lessons"; *The Bridge:* "For Rachel" and "The
Blind Man,"; *The Chariton Review:* "Driving the Cattle Home"; *Embers:* "The
Lady Next Door"; *The Formalist:* "Snow Globe"; *Hellas:* "Christmas at the
Airport"; *Hiram Poetry Review:* "For Rilke, For Us," "The Wall, " "Even
Now" (as "Meditation"), "The Film, " "What She Knew," and "Beet
Weeding"; *The Journal:* "Another Life, " "The Roar, " and "The Fever"; *The
Madison Review:* "Failure"; *The New Criterion:* "An Old New England
Graveyard"; *The New Review:* "The Fisher" and "On Meaning"; *Partisan
Review:* "Now and Then"; *Peregrine:* "Gone South"; *The Poetry Review
(PSA):* "The Puzzle"; and *The Widener Review:* "Sounding the Quarry" and
"Men Lying Awake."

"Just" appeared in *The 1997 Anthology of Magazine Verse & Yearbook of
American Poetry.*

The author wishes to thank Yaddo and The Millay Colony for fellowships
that provided valuable time to generate many of these poems.

Special thanks to Gene Zeiger, Susan Roeper, Milt Djuric, Dennis Johnson,
and Lawrence Raab for their comments and criticism over the years, as well
as to Ted Deppe, Amy Dryansky, Paul Jenkins, Mary Koncel, and Ellen
Watson.

Manufactured in the United States of America

Orchises Press
P. O. Box 20602
Alexandria
Virginia
22320-1602

G6E4C2A

for *Susan*

CONTENTS

I

II

We say ourselves in syllables that rise
From the floor, rising in speech we do not speak.

WHAT SHE KNEW

I

SNOW GLOBE

The little girl stands
inside her element
forever on tiptoe
mailing her present

to someone somewhere
past a clear wall
wishing wishing
for snow to fall

in flakes that settle
like an afterthought
inside a world shaken
where she stands caught

in the urge for release
wound up in a bow
the little girl sends
through drifting snow.

THE FEVER

I was the fire
in a summer's afternoon.
I heard the small birds speak:
re-peat, re-peat, they said
from under brushwood, beyond
the curtain's muggy wind
that worked the bed sheets,
broke over my skin
with wave on spilling wave
of furnace heat.

Then woke to darkness,
black and big and wet
with the sweet salt rush,
the sudden sweat
of absolution
and the knowledge won
each time I felt the pulse
that beat and beat
the little bloody drum
inside my chest.

LESSONS

for Rick

I

Somehow it became "my thirtieth year to heaven"
that day in school I first read Dylan Thomas.
The assignment: memorize a famous poem,
recite it, don't giggle, somehow try to ignore
your best friend's screwed-up face, his broken promise.

Eyes fixed on the back wall, feet surveying the floor
for a crevice or canyon where I could disappear,
I stammered on through it, toppling each line's hurdle

—till suddenly I was there—transformed and able:
the room, the class, their silent punitive laughter
erased and forgotten; my best friend's smirking face
turned serious, and everything I knew
seeming small and curious in that altered air.

II

I remember the store clerk, glasses pinching her nose,
my embarrassed shuffle in grass-stained tennis shoes
while handing her the book—the first I chose
out of hunger: Hemingway's *For Whom the Bell Tolls*,
the Scribner edition that boasted a flashy cover
of a war scene, soldiers, hills, the exploding rose
a bomb made deep in night. . .

                    and how I froze
as if before the jury or my first imagined lover,
when, finishing the book, I scratched a reddish blotch
I thought a bomb-burst, then found that it was blood:

17

and me sixteen, the summer long and hot
with revelation, this burning I understood
to be at the core of all the books I read,
the strange, mercurial things they left unsaid.

III

Chatter and small talk peppered the diamond.
At night our voices cheered the home team on
beneath the arc lamps, a rounded platinum moon
floating high above the crowd that gathered
and leaped to a roar the moment they hit one out
or nailed the tag, the runner charging from third
spikes up into the plate and that dusty shout
of "Outta hee-ah!" we loved to shower down.

Then later, much later, the echoed crack and pop
of consonant and vowel slapped out by the keys,
me down in the cellar trying to write it up,
crouched low and dug in, squinting to see
noun slide into verb, the perfect strike,
a sentence sent sailing across the page at night.

THE WALL

for Peter Carpenter

In the morning the wall
we'd built from various stones
stood somehow changed
by sunlight in the garden,
the morning dew, and the air
cool from the valley and clear.

For what was clear
was that our wall,
as if out of thin air,
had become more than its stones,
more than just a shape in the garden
to organize the weeds. It had changed

because how we saw it had changed,
standing there in the patch we'd cleared.
What had simply been a neglected garden
now contained our wall,
larger, more wobbly, than any stone.
Way off in the valley the air

lay open as air,
grassy, wild, unchanged.
There the fields were scattered with stones.
But was our field a field more clear
because divided, set off by our wall?
Or was it simply our garden?

Answers grow poorly in gardens.
It has something to do with the air.
Yet for all its bulk, the idea of our wall
had brought us a delicate change.

The flowers less wild, more clear
in their reds and greens on the stone,

somehow something strange, not of stone,
had crept out in the midst of our garden.
How sad, how clear
it felt there in the early air.
Everything around us was changed.
For what had been our wall

was clearly now a part of the garden,
destined to change in the air
from garden to wall to stone.

An Old New England Graveyard

At the field's far end, down by
the dredged and roaring stream,
past alleys of long light reaching
through windbreak maple and beech
to scrape an old barn ruddy
despite its sagging loft,
he finds them:
                    Headstones and
their heavings, those we label
"forgotten and ignored,"
as if we could forget them,
the dead, and all their trappings.

Listless, historical, bored—
no doubt they do not mind
the gate's low groan when opened
by the odd man out in spring,
who, there among the weeds,
the names, the graven phrase
or two, might find himself
reduced to those low whispers
of "Gardner, Doty, Nash...,"

Or, considering the past,
hears in his own heart's knocking
the windy present beat,
takes measure of the stones,
makes note of their mossy touch,
straddles the tufted grass,
closes the gate, and goes home.

SOUNDING THE QUARRY

Abandoned now, I hardly think of it
except as out of the way, where the road bends
sharp by the overhead trolley that used to carry
limestone down the hillside, above the traffic,
toppling it with a crash into yawning bins.

Itching for a walk, maybe once a summer
I head on up the back road, veering off
onto the crushed stone stretch that starts out
wide and inviting, before it narrows soon
to a weedy lane, the end of which then opens

onto the waste beds, piled up scattered mounds
of furnace silt trucked back up the hill
and dumped here. After many years of weather
the landscape's softened, white moguls rolling
which lately local kids with leaping skill

have mastered with their bikes, wild mid-air turns
and wheelies accomplished to the mounting dares
until, inevitably, a tire lands wrong, skids out,
someone's sent sailing over handlebars and home
to patch a bloodied knee, hide tears with winces.

Crazed circles in the dust, their tracks surround
the switching tower, where once the weight of a truck
my father drove geared down its heavy load,
dumped it quick, his skin made grey as ash
when later he'd come home covered with the silt.

Though it's all boarded up, sealed off for good,
I always stop a while beside the tower,
enjoying somehow the ghostly way it rises

above the sun-blanched dust, disconnected
electric wires splayed out like bent antennas

receiving echoes and rumblings, grunts and laughter
mixed with the shudder of lumbering ore cars
spit out by the nearby tunnel, and how I hear
the calls for more material, orders snapped,
cuss words muttered back on whiskey breath,

the excited noon-time whistle. After that
it's up the steeper hill, by now the sun
hotter yet with each locust's rising whine,
my leisurely step turned laborious, purposeful,
breath shortening with the grade, here and there

the startled rustle of a bird or squirrel
breaking the trance, the stillness of my thoughts
lost to the sky and woods, since most of the way
there's nothing really to think about or see,
nothing but stone and sand along the road.

I'm never ready. Never quite ready for
the sucking reel of space—empty, crystalline—
that looms up white from what must surely be
a half mile opposite, the plunging cliffs
ragged now with moss and spilling vines,

yet dizzying still. . . Or what it does to me
to come upon that place, stare down and think
of men creating unwittingly, year by year,
this blown-up patch of time, this negative
of toil and sweat and stone and honest hope

collapsing into the earth, where at the bottom
a tiny stream now winds its way through swamp,
traveling God knows where to spill itself,

made manifest perhaps when the last pick dropped,
the whistle blew its final call, somewhere

someone closed a window, set the kettle on,
began to peel potatoes, the weary ashen figures
of father and friends carrying empty lunch pails
back down the sloping hillside, while farther off
gathering clouds brought on a soft cool rain.

And yet somehow I'm drawn here, sounding the quarry
with a stone or two sent whistling, whistling
down through the throaty air. Though I never see
them land, something in the muffled pock they make
reveals the swampy bottom, and how they got there,

balancing the weight of trucks, of families, bills,
the lost back pay; while with each stone let go,
the seconds it takes to hit, I carry away
something discovered in the arc that drops
that's weightless, familiar—then plummeting, a gift.

HIDDEN MEADOW

Moss Phlox. Cinquefoil. Bluet. Aven.
Sheep Sorrel. Hawkweed. Dense Blazing Star.
All the way across wildflowers kept me
afloat and sailing, lost

in a dream of equilibrium, the landscape
liquid, yet intractable as glacial drift;
the meadow's polyglot surface swimming up.
Rose-pink. Forget-me-not.

JUST

Like the patch of violets
that appears just as the lawn
has gotten out of hand
each spring, the daffodils,
just having lost their petals,
toss in the breeze outside
the window that holds a view
where nothing in particular
happens, just a boat
that scarcely seems to sway
on the lake, its surface just
barely disturbed, just lovely
after last night's storm—
just what I meant to tell you.

FOR RACHEL

Born yesterday, the first of spring
saw you arrive to snow and cold,
your sudden life, its happening,
asleep and tiny in the blanket's folds.

Down the windy, snow-swept streets
mothers lugged children, traffic crept;
somewhere quite elsewhere a hospital sheet
settled on one who, faltering, slept.

But you, sweet little new one,
inside your fleshy comfort curled,
know only the milk-fed safe oblivion
of this your first day's first felt world.

Snug, tiny bud, I wish you nothing,
nothing but *presence* in what you pass:
snow on parked cars, houses at evening,
one's breath against a pane of glass.

NOW AND THEN

JAMES MERRILL (1926-1995)

Midway through this morning
a helicopter throbs,
disrupting a cloudless sky
that lights the downward look
I've cast, once more, with pleasure
into the pages of your book.

It's June, four months later
on that installment plan
we all sign up for, now and then
remembrance demanding we pay
the bill, remit our loss,
your "Farewell Performance" that day

a detour on the syllabus
sadly taken, then embraced
in the hope that you'd reprise
us with your brilliant act,
though knowing, gentle conjurer,
all magic ends in fact.

Or does it? Above, the chopper
whirs. I can feel its pulse
press the canopy of leaves
pliant as a damask curtain
that, sweeping back, reveals
a child to a world of passions

rehearsed in the home he feels
as rigged as it is broken,
where Wotan's stormy bass,
Brünnhilde on the pyre

threaten to engulf him,
but don't, becoming the fire

that lit your art from within
its self-sustaining flame:
opera, child, curtain,
loss, an open book—
all fair game in the consuming
glance, the upward look

that hovers here this morning,
wiser, no less scattered,
knowing life the richer for you
and. . . look, a glint of sun?
no, wait. . . the pilot's waving!
as he passes and is gone.

II

SUMMER STORM

Lights flickering out at 4 p.m.,
there's nothing left to do
but watch the approaching storm

move in, obscure the view,
creating a neutral stain
of gray and black on blue

that lowers like a curtain,
with first fat drops that hiss,
onto the ragged mountain

of open-throated lilies,
stippled black on orange beyond
the pane, and the thought of this.

DRIVING THE CATTLE HOME

after Brueghel

This is the turning from summer,
cattle at day's end climbing
up from low pasture,
the cowherd's heavy stick
prodding them slowly home.

Nearby, the peasant workers
bend over the tawny soil,
their weathered fingers
harvesting the baron's wheat
as he follows the lumbering herd

on horseback, contemplating dinner,
despite the darkening clouds
that shadow the river
below those ice blue mountains
that promise an early snow.

"Wine, then sleep," thinks the baron,
as the cowherd lowers his prod
to cut the escape
of that white and jittery cow,
as it pauses, turns, and disappears.

CHRISTMAS AT THE AIRPORT

Their round mouths pucker to a chorus *O*...
it's good to see you,
                    as the plane unloads,
dispatching daughters, sons, and grans to crowds
of yearly hugs and kisses.

                    Outside, the snow
settles as backdrop for the muted No-el,
No-el piped in above the idling Fords,
their engines purring like a Lord's prayer
muttered softly.

                Then quietly they go,
moving as one along the polished hallway.
The baggage found, the family flocked together,

they exit to the car, the local weather
chilly and bright above their lifted eyes,
their swift and heavy bodies
                        crossing the ice.

MEN LYING AWAKE

stumble down the hallways of their lives,
   know that the past's exotic flora,
green and breathing within the humid dark,

lie in a room locked up, walled in by glass
   damp with moisture they cannot touch,
despite the tall plants swaying, a little wind

busying the leaves, the dew, the impeccable flowers
   just beyond the pane reflecting
the moonlight's metallic chill—end of the hall,

middle of winter, as a car starts up outside,
   a neighbor guns his engine, drives
off in a cloud of steam through the pre-dawn cold.

TRAVELING IN AMERICA

Begin in Arkansas
and travel north,
through Iowa, the Badlands,
the erasure of a whiteout
anticipating the blank
stare of the Boise waitress,

coffee steaming the small talk
of crops and pickups
made at the local saloon,
where Broad Betty sucks
her beer down quick as lightning
over the Pacific

in a storm off Puget Sound,
the arc of your headlights
licking the salt mist
as you turn south
and drive towards Sacramento,
sunshine and smog

thick as the gospel lowing
heard on the radio
outside of L.A.,
the low rider rumble
of Chicano Chevies cruising
the ghetto streets,

dashboards lit up like the horizon
of the desert in twilight
your map labels Nevada,
Arizona, New Mexico. . .
but which may seem "Delirium,"
a state of mind

you cross, nonetheless knowing
it's a pointless,
and therefore, beautiful journey,
America being
a large country full of nothing
but the gossip

of chattering neighbors
outside of Houston,
Baton Rouge, Mobile, Savannah,
where there is nothing
you could hope to see or understand
unless you stopped

for a spell and listened in
on the lazy drawl
or Yankee clip by which
the story is told
about the gunman in Arkansas,
or in Albany,

the long arm of the law
out to skin his hide
in Bangor or in Akron,
hunting him down
inside a Tulsa warehouse,
an Omaha barn,

or right here in the desert,
your eyes ignoring
the arms of that stranded driver
flagging you down,
alone and helpless, knowing
he's one of us.

THE FILM

Late in autumn it occurs to him:
sunlight pouring off the lake and past
tasseled curtains that drape the study windows
creates now a continuous film, a single frame
of light wavering across the wall and up
onto the ceiling, like a projector running empty

after a double matinee, a few lost souls
with nothing better to do than see a movie
hanging on for just a minute longer,
until, embarrassed by the screen's white blaze,
they decide to leave, exiting one by one
into the city, its traffic, its grainy light.

THE BLIND MAN

So much is unexpected. Whole rooms I've mapped
to memory—ashtray on the mantelpiece,
whiskey by the lamp—have disassembled;
their everyday arrangement swept and altered
by a guest in conversation who, unthinking,
might go on and on about the job, the marriage,
the island vacation, another divorce, then set
the bottle down—left of the lamp, not right—
while all God's children cannot bring it back
till I bump its amber shape.

                      But you, my friend,
—Another? Thanks. No ice. I'll have it neat.—
seem different, stopping in to visit, an edge
to your neighborly chat, which coupled now
with this ungodly question—What's it like to. . . ?—
has me guessing that you're looking for advice;
the makeup of my world, its familiar dark,
perhaps if thoroughly explained, telling you
how to move through life unbruised, unbroken,
escaping each small harm.

                     How disappointing.
I simply live, you see, anticipating
no more than my own allotted share
of pained confusion—visions and prophecy,
all that bad press regarding special gifts
being just another blindness in itself,
while this I'll tell you now: there is no pity
in the misplaced cane, the broken glass or two.
The pity's something larger, something shared
between us: it's forgetting what or who
set off that special echoing inside your head,
for when you later try to haul it up

while swimming in that inky dark, but can't,
why then you're truly lost.

                           For instance take
that wife of yours. Out in the yard, across
our shared low fence, I think I've come to know
how beautiful she is: those loving hands,
their gentle touch—Sure, go ahead, please smoke—
the smile that's in her words. However, do you?
For if you cannot see just who she is,
she'll not see you, or maybe start to think
the marriage long dried up, cold and dead,
until one day while picking up the kids
she'll see a cloud, adjust her rearview mirror,
discover it there no matter where she turns
—that grey, ambiguous puff hovering within
the glass, and all she's ever loved or known
afloat and fading, belonging to the past.

It is one thing to see—hand me that bottle—
it's another thing yet to know what lies before you.
The tender kiss? The shy, suggestive smile?
Perhaps a special meal served up with candles
when you least expect it? All quite ordinary
I hear you nod and smugly say—but not
so quick.

                What happens if you hear beyond
the pleasant chatter or the warmth within
that after-dinner sigh? What do you do
when suddenly alone, unable to sleep, you think
where does she go? who does she meet? as around you
the house sits black and breathing, headlights roam
the walls, when gradually it comes to you
—it's him! she really loves the guy!—his hands,
I mean, or from across the crowded ballroom
that pencil-thin sharp laugh you always thought

ridiculous, almost a handicap, but now
the one that haunts you, echoing and echoing
in all that roomy black.

                              I see you're stirring.
Perhaps I've touched a nerve. My friend, relax,
go home, sit down in darkness, listen close.
What you will hear just resting there will be
all you can ask to know. The heart's deep thrum,
the ticking of your pulse, what you remember
of how she brushed her hair, or how long it's been
since, whispering her name, you looked within
her eyes and saw that world that neither moves
nor ages, if only to discover how much it does
and did.

            The house, the wife, the sleeping kids
might seem just that—an orderly rented life,
while you alone are left to listen to the dark,
find a path, a lane through the haunted woods,
without which you and I and we are lost,
condemned to long for what we once were given,
all that we're not—or if it's ever lost,
to know it, my friend, remember that it's gone.

THE FISHER

Long it had been rumored in this province:
part weasel, part otter—something silvery
slithering on lakeshores down among the rocks.

Some put it down as error, others the return
of a species we thought for decades had abandoned
our local woods and water for regions north,

where in forests of pine, old wives' tales told,
lay danger to children, those who misbehaved,
carried off nightly, never seen again.

Then you, your hair done up against the heat,
legs propped on the dash as we drove home,
saying Stop! Stop! out on the narrow causeway

we were crossing, then crossed, the two of us
convinced, enamored: the arching, bush-like tail,
lithe, slippery body, though later we told no one.

BEET WEEDING

"Why don't you weed the beets," she said, suggesting
that I leave her to the spinach on her own
so she could finish, maybe work on dinner.
"Besides, you're still a learner," she slyly added,
prodding my backside with the hoe's blunt handle,
both of us knowing, as she turned and left me
to liberate the beets from their lowly weed-dom,
my gardening know-how so much less than hers.

How right she was I soon discovered, myself
a novice fool who thought that kneeling down
with each June beet (like any squash or sprout)
and combing one by one would turn our patch
into an open ordered plain, an army
on the march, with all that tousling green
like some crusade sent headlong row by row
into the teeth of August.

                              "Silly," she said,
"You've got to weed them out, not just spruce up
the bed like some showpiece for *Gardener's Monthly*.
Look at the package!" as she advised and read,
pointing a muddy finger. *"When plants are five
to six inches tall, remove each second one
(preferably the weaker sort) in order that
enough space lies between (about four inches)
for rest to thrive and grow—*'Cause if you don't
we'll have no beets at all, but just a heap
of crowded bitter greens."

                              I simply didn't know,
as she went off across the yard and in
to clang, chop, boil, and sizzle at our dinner,
that gardening could come down to this. One beet

condemned because too close for comfort to
a neighbor, while all the guides so calmly wrote:
*The best means to avoid attrition. Saves space
and guarantees a crop as well.* As if
some beet might nod approval—quiver, shake,
then see the common good.

                        Like some thick god,
I bent and worked alone as evening fell
across the hillside, field, and river,
then heard her call and saw her wave me in
to quit, wash up, help her set the table.
"Lesson learned?" she asked and smiled, arranging
the flowers, plates, and silver; as I sat down
beet-dazed and weary, and told her that I loved her.

RENEWAL

for Jan & David

Like a skein of geese that winds its way
about a mottled sky, first wheeling north
towards the inland pond whose wintry knowledge
is skimmed with ice, then banking west, across
a ruddy sunset before the turn to south,

we choose our journeys by indirection's course,
deciding what flight to take by the one fogged in,
connections made or lost, the discount fare
that gets you there, no less loved, and home.

For like responsibilities, distances connect
and reconnect us, compassing a need
for what we've known, be it old friends,
a favorite chair, or as with geese, desire
for return compelling us suddenly skyward,

a garland of distress that honks and shudders,
then finds familiar shape in the arrowed V
that occurs mid-flight, and is a vow, is renewal,
something that we make, then remake once again.

And so, like vows, each journey's charted end
lies as far beyond us as beginning—or if
discovered, accidental, a coin that's tossed
into a pond in autumn, whose surface stirring
replenishes our need to pause, reflect

on waters troubling, traveling to each shore,
and like us, caught up in headlong flight,
since by such longing we remain discernible,
unlike the wheeling geese in the wheeling sky.

III

FOR RILKE, FOR US

And you, who never stopped believing
the pain of roses, wooden chairs, cupboards
laid bare to their spaces, and evening
brought down to a star. What would you tell?

Nights I hear them, voices answering back,
somewhere something said and lost to hope
beneath the summer porches, somewhere close
as rain and a woman washing her hair.

Gone, she will return. There at the window
to calm the feverish child, to settle
the day's disorder of things, then back
downstairs again to tea and weariness.

Everywhere they die and everywhere they live,
"and it's hard being dead," you said, well knowing
the loss is in between what was and is
the risk of angels in a world of men.

Late, hours have passed. The woman dries her hair;
outside the air is wet with noise
as, restless for a walk as she turns in, I step
into the street to find that this is where we are.

THE ROAR

for Jan & Jamie

I've heard the sea is a sensible place to die,
that, drowning there, one becomes so quickly lost
among the stars and fishes, laboring tides,
kelp and pirate's gold.

Others say the sea is mere abstraction,
a tale we tell ourselves to entertain an urge
for matters beyond knowing, its bitter salt
no more than a mythic lie.

Old moon, old conspiracy
of light and dark shining in a gravedigger sky,
you will have to tell me. I am miles inland,
I own no map, and cannot sleep in the roar.

GONE SOUTH

Warm winter rain while driving home tonight,
slush under the tires replacing hard-packed snow,
makes this December seem like a damp Havana
although I've never been there.

                       Palm trees, a stroll
along some evening avenue with a sultry girl,
a café's yellow wash of light, its smoky rumba
thumps back and forth across my foggy windshield,

the grinding, slow
                     efforts of the worn out blades
to carve their double arch, two tunnelled holes
into the future.

              For I've gone south for winter,
leaving behind this town of traffic and brick,
where two streets back this guy pulls out and hits
the brakes barely in time

                  for me to imagine
the skid and crash, the fiery display
of rescue lights across the nestled houses,
faces at windows squinting concern,

                   before I swerve
and sail on safe, my mind adrift and dreaming
about a country where I've never been,
where the revolution is bloodless, everyone free.

BELIEF

It's like an old cistern you come upon
in new growth forest, the map's worn path
dead ending where three streamlets meet
beneath bowed saplings to mix and form

a pool's glassed surface, its shallow depth
now silted in around the standing pipe
that filters the run off, feeds it through
to the buried cistern's brick-lined dark.

Bending down, it might occur to you
to inspect the cover's mossy weight
that with a grunt you lift, surprised
by your own reflection staring up,

cut off and bobbing in the leafy sky,
while out of nowhere a bead of sweat
sets rings, like questions, rippling out
across the surface, prodding you to ask,

Where does the water go? Is there someone
living down the hill who still depends
on gravity to feed an icy tap?
Someone who, in reaching out,

need only turn a spigot's brass
to know pure water always there
and never drought? Someone, sometime
must have thought to work it out

and built the cistern, maybe causing you
to settle its cover with a careful thud,
returning home a little more amazed
than when you found it, long out of use,

the echoing thrum inside its chamber
rendered historical on the folded map,
though like any old lie, subterraneous,
and if discovered, slaking your thirst.

EVEN NOW

for Ilona & Neil

Everything happens for a reason;
in this the deception of fate.
How, for instance, late
last night while watching
stars through a telescope's lens
we spoke about each of us
having this need to see
patterns of our making
stripped clean and broken down
to a mythic simpleness,

while, even now, the blue
unalterable sky reflected
in the watery sway and lap
of light that cleanses pine,
this morning's mottled birch,
has nothing but its own
symmetry to explain
its placid, balanced beauty,
or what we call illusion.

So, too, with hope and pain
among the many thousands.
And so with friendship, even love,
beneath those constellations
ironic and short-lived,
instructing our whispered talk
there in the marginal dark
of the full moon's mounting drift
as it clears the hill's black rim,
rises, and is seen, and is.

ON MEANING

It's not that the snow outside
sifting down through pine
where a tufted sparrow flits
should correspond in any way
to the man who is inside thinking

that snow is an intricate message
about the reticence of winter,
since only a habit of meaning
argues the falling snow
has something to do with the man,

the sparrow, his quiet breathing.

WHAT SHE KNEW

Self-portraiture obsessed her, the problem being
to find someone she could trust to photograph
her glance from sudden angles that would reveal
knowledge, like water, that she hoped to paint.

Later in the darkroom, wrongness floated up,
the photo snapped too fast, out of focus,
herself mis-caught, mis-taken, and nothing for it
but to try to paint what she knew existed, felt

in the sway and toss of heavy-headed flowers
outside her window, trumpeting their name.

FAILURE

In that classic argument that breaks out over
the table's being there or not—lingering halos
of cool wet drinks that confess to beaded trembling
when a neighbor slaps the surface, insists his take
the only true one on the matter—try thinking
of failure.

One look at history, for instance,
would argue that, without failure, we'd be nowhere.
Great revolutions, crusades for God or bread
have leveled entire mountains to escape
boredom in the palace, as the sleepy king,
whose ring-laden fingers drum absent-mindedly
the throne's carved mermaid, considers the queen's
indifference of late, while outside in the garden
he hears trilled animation in her voice,
observes the bobbing head and sees it lean,
consumed with the bearded tutor.

It's then failure
can erupt like influenza, breeding in the king
an appetite for towns, the charred feeling
of betrayal roiling his stomach like tainted oysters,
or later, and probable, from behind a curtain
the tutor leaping, quick as a knife, to launch
the famous coup.

Likewise, failure can instruct,
being, in retrospect, a kind of culmination
of our bad beginnings and hurried plans now read
as *should haves, could haves* that strangely keep us
addicted to what's possible—sunlight seen
from the cliffs, reflecting off a coral reef
that just beneath an ambling wave appears,

then disappears, the sea's occluding drift
confirming the loss of what was surely there
and now we find hard to know.

                              On the other hand,
there's Admiral Scott, lost to antarctic wastes,
who could have spent those last days cursing Amundsen,
but instead chose wonder, to record the facts,
the wind from N. to N.W. and -40 temp. . . ,
drift snow like finest flour. . . the small green tent
and the great white road. . . the horses dying,
tragedy all along the line.

                              There in silence,
was it failure that fed the ember of his thought
flickering, flickering before it fluttered out,
or was it something else, *half a pannikin*
of cocoa cooked over the spirit, absurd, pathetic,
and hidden within, that caused him then to write
for God's sake look after our people. . . ?

                              Failure
instructs, and is a godsend, numbering our days
with assurances at twilight of all we know:
fading, roseate light on a dusk-edged meadow,
as evening threads its way slowly through the trees,
and your neighbor relaxes, his leisurely position
there, across the table, a shadow that stands
between the two of you, and failing that,
impossible to see.

THE LADY NEXT DOOR

As the blue rain begins to fall and the pink
azaleas are everywhere wet with what
comes down and soaks the smoking hatless man
beneath the wooden eaves, where children run
to escape the puddles while the trees unbend
above the grasses and the swallows disappear;
she opens the window and calls to them, screaming
for the children to get out of their muddy socks,
for the man to come in with his pipe
since she must clean the house and hasn't forever
to yell at them for being so foolish
as to stand around watching the trees
sway in the wind, and the flowers fall to pieces,
while they catch their death of cold in the rain.

THE PUZZLE

for Leslie

So you've done the puzzle,
tamping down each tiny piece
of azure sky, the lake's black mirror,
where for a day, the clouds
are doubled as clouds, captured
and perfected in their nature.

Though that's a habit of nature,
it creates the worst of puzzles.
How, for instance, what's captured
alone in a single piece
can remain as much a cloud
as it can a mirror.

True, only an intricate mirror
can reflect the jigsaw of nature,
but to see a cloud as cloud
is really the crux of the puzzle.
Otherwise, in the confusion of pieces,
we remain as captured

as those pines are mysteriously captured,
windless and cold in the mirror.
And yet, when fingering the pieces,
what within your nature
drew you to such a puzzle?
Beyond the cumulus clouds,

maybe those other clouds
of doubt or the future captured
your heart and made it a puzzle,
revealing a tear in the mirror?

Or was it simply that nature
beckoned the urge to piece

together a habitable peace,
there in the morning clouds?
Either way, it's nature,
human, disordered, or captured,
which by setting the scope of the mirror
still limits the frame of the puzzle.

ANOTHER LIFE

floats on the wind
outside my window,
a storm advancing
on tall bent trees,

where children run
at sunset across
the new mown grass
as the sky shifts pink

to grey in the painting
of a woman who stands
naked in a room,
nothing before her

but the immediate city,
and just beyond
what she knew
was sky, was open sea.